OCS Report
MMS 2009-042

Investigation of Fatality from Falling Load
Main Pass Block 30, Well No. A-14 ST01
OCS-G 4903
7 March 2009

Gulf of Mexico
Off the Louisiana Coast

U.S. Department of the Interior
Minerals Management Service
Gulf of Mexico OCS Regional Office

New Orleans
July 2009

OCS Report
MMS 2009-042

Investigation of Fatality from Falling Load
Main Pass Block 30, Well No. A-14 ST01
OCS-G 4903
7 March 2009

Gulf of Mexico
Off the Louisiana Coast

Glynn T. Breaux – Chair
Randy Josey
David Emilien

U.S. Department of the Interior
Minerals Management Service
Gulf of Mexico OCS Regional Office

New Orleans
July 2009

Contents

List of Figures

List of Tables

Abbreviations and Acronyms

Air tugger	(air-operated hoist)
ALARP	As Low As Reasonably Practicable
ASAP	As Soon as Possible
BHA	Bottom Hole Assembly
BOPE	Blowout Preventer Equipment
Chevron	(Chevron U.S.A., Inc.)
Chevron's Handbook	(Chevron's GOM Business Units Shelf and Deepwater Contractor's Handbook – Revised January 2008)
CIBP	Cast Iron Bridge Plug
CPR	Cardio Pulmonary Resuscitation
Driller	Hercules Offshore Rig 120 Driller
FH-1	Hercules Offshore Rig 120 Floor Hand No. 1 (the Deceased)
FH-2	Hercules Offshore Rig 120 Floor Hand No. 2
FH-3	Hercules Offshore Rig 120 Floor Hand No. 3
FIT	Formation Integrity Test
Flow Chart	(Events/Causal Factor Diagram of the Accident)
GOM	Gulf of Mexico
GR-CCL	Gamma Ray-Casing Collar Locator
HCR	Remotely Operated Hydraulic Control Valve
HO	Hercules Offshore Rig 120 Hoist Operator
HSE	Health, Environmental and Safety
IV	(Intravenous fluids)
JHA	Job Hazard Analysis
JSA	Job Safety Analysis
MES	Multi-Linear Event Sequence Diagram
MMS	Minerals Management Service
MOL	Move on Location
MP	Main Pass
ND	Nipple-Down
NU	Nipple-Up

OCS	Outer Continental Shelf
OIM	Hercules Offshore Installation Manager/Licensed Master (Captain) in command of a liftboat
OSHA	Occupational Safety and Health Administration
OSM	(MMS Regional Office of Safety Management)
PPE	Personal Protective Equipment
ppg	pounds per gallon
PIC	Person-in-Charge
POOH	Pull Out of Hole
SBM	Synthetic Base Mud
SLS	Secondary Load Support
Subpart O	(MMS 30 CFR Part 250, Subpart O training requirements)
SWA	Stop Work Authority
SWL	Maximum Safe Working Load
T&A'd	Temporarily Abandoned
The rig	(Hercules Offshore Rig 120)
The well	(Main Pass Block 30, Lease OCS-G 4903 Well No. A-14 ST01)
TIH	Trip in Hole
USCG	United States Coast Guard
VETCO	(Established in July 2004 through subsidiaries Vetco Gray and Abiel. Vetco Gray was sold to General Electric on January 9, 2007)

Executive Summary

An accident that resulted in one fatality and an injury occurred on the Hercules Offshore Rig 120 (the rig) contracted by Chevron USA Inc. (Chevron) to conduct sidetracking operations from Lease OCS-G-4903, Main Pass (MP) Block 30, Well No. A-14 ST01 (the well), in the Gulf of Mexico (GOM) offshore Louisiana, on 7 March 2009 at approximately 2158 hours. Lifting operations from the rig floor were in progress utilizing the rig floor air tugger (air-operated hoist) to position a 2- inch rubber hose, with internal steel construction rated for high pressure, for testing the well's 13-3/8 inch x 9-7/8 inch casing annulus. The fifty (50) feet, approximately 400 pounds, of hose assembly was lowered from the rig floor to the wellhead deck where the lower end of the hose assembly would be connected into the well's 13-3/8 inch x 9-7/8 inch casing annulus valve and the upper end of the hose assembly connected to the rig floor manifold. Subsequent to lowering the hose assembly from the rig floor to near the wellhead deck, it was determined that the 50 feet of hose assembly failed to reach the well's annular casing valve by approximately 10 feet. At this time the Hercules Offshore Hoist Operator (Hoist Operator) began to retrieve the hose assembly back into the derrick above the rig floor where it could be swapped-out with 100 feet of hose section that was located on one wall of the rig floor. The lift connection being used was comprised of a WECO Figure 1502 hammer union that had been previously modified by the addition of a welded bale. When the 50 feet of hose assembly was lifted approximately 30 feet into the derrick above the rig floor, the lift connection failed just above the weld on one end of the bale. The Hercules Offshore Floor Hand No. 1 (FH-1), standing near the center of the rig floor but not directly under the assembly, received life threatening injuries (unresponsive but breathing) subsequent to being struck on the top of his hardhat by the hose assembly. The hose assembly then continued its descent from the rig floor's edge through the rig's air gap and next to the wellhead deck into the GOM. The Hercules Offshore Rig Floor Hand No. 2 (FH-2), standing next to the hand railing on the rig floor and manipulating the hose to protect the load from snagging on any protrusions, was initially knocked down by the hose. FH-2 arose to move away from the rig floor railing, only to be knocked down again by the air-operated hoist wire rope that back-lashed subsequent to the loss of the load's weight. FH-2 sustained a superficial laceration to his right triceps with right shoulder pain.

The Minerals Management Service (MMS) accident investigation Panel concluded that the accident was preventable. The **Cause** of the 7 March 2009 accident was the use of a modified WECO Figure 1502 hammer union that failed just above the weld on one end of the welded bale. **Possible Contributing**

Causes include: (1) improper monitoring of the Hercules Offshore equipment inspection program, (2) lift crew location during the bulk hose lifting operation, (3) the lack of a formal written Job Safety Analysis (JSA) to accompany the pre-job lift safety meeting and (4) JSA policy oversight by rig management.

Introduction

Authority

A fatal accident and injury occurred on 7 *March 2009* at approximately *2158 hours* aboard the jack-up drilling rig Hercules Offshore Rig 120 (the rig) contracted to Chevron USA Inc. (Chevron) while operations were being conducted on Lease OCS-G 4903, Main Pass (MP) Block 30, Well No. A-14 ST01 (the well), in the Gulf of Mexico (GOM) offshore Louisiana.

The fatally injured person was a Hercules Offshore Floor Hand (FH-1) employee. At the time of the accident FH-1 was observing a bulk hose lifting operation from the near the center of the rig floor but not directly under the hose assembly. FH-1 had just changed positions with another Hercules Offshore Floor Hand (FH-2) who was standing next to the rig floor hand rail and manipulating the hose to protect the load from snagging on any protrusions.

Pursuant to 43 U.S.C. 1348(d)(1) and (2) and (f) [Outer Continental Shelf (OCS) Lands Act, as amended] and Department of the Interior regulations 30 CFR 250, the Minerals Management Service (MMS) is required to investigate and prepare a report of this accident. By memorandum dated 13 March 2009, the following personnel were named to the investigative panel:

> Glynn T. Breaux, Chairman – Office of Safety Management, Field Operations, GOM OCS Region
> Randy Josey – Office of Safety Management, Field Operations, GOM OCS Region
> David Emilien – New Orleans District, Field Operations, GOM OCS Region

Background

Lease OCS-G 4903 covers approximately 5,000 acres and is located in Main Pass Block 30, Gulf of Mexico, off the Louisiana Coast (*see Figure 1*). The lease was purchased by seven (7) original Lessees in Sale Number 66, with an effective lease date of 1 December 1981 and a first producing lease date of 28 November 1987. Chevron U.S.A. Inc. is the record title interest owner effective 8 August 2005 and became designated operator on 21 June 2006.

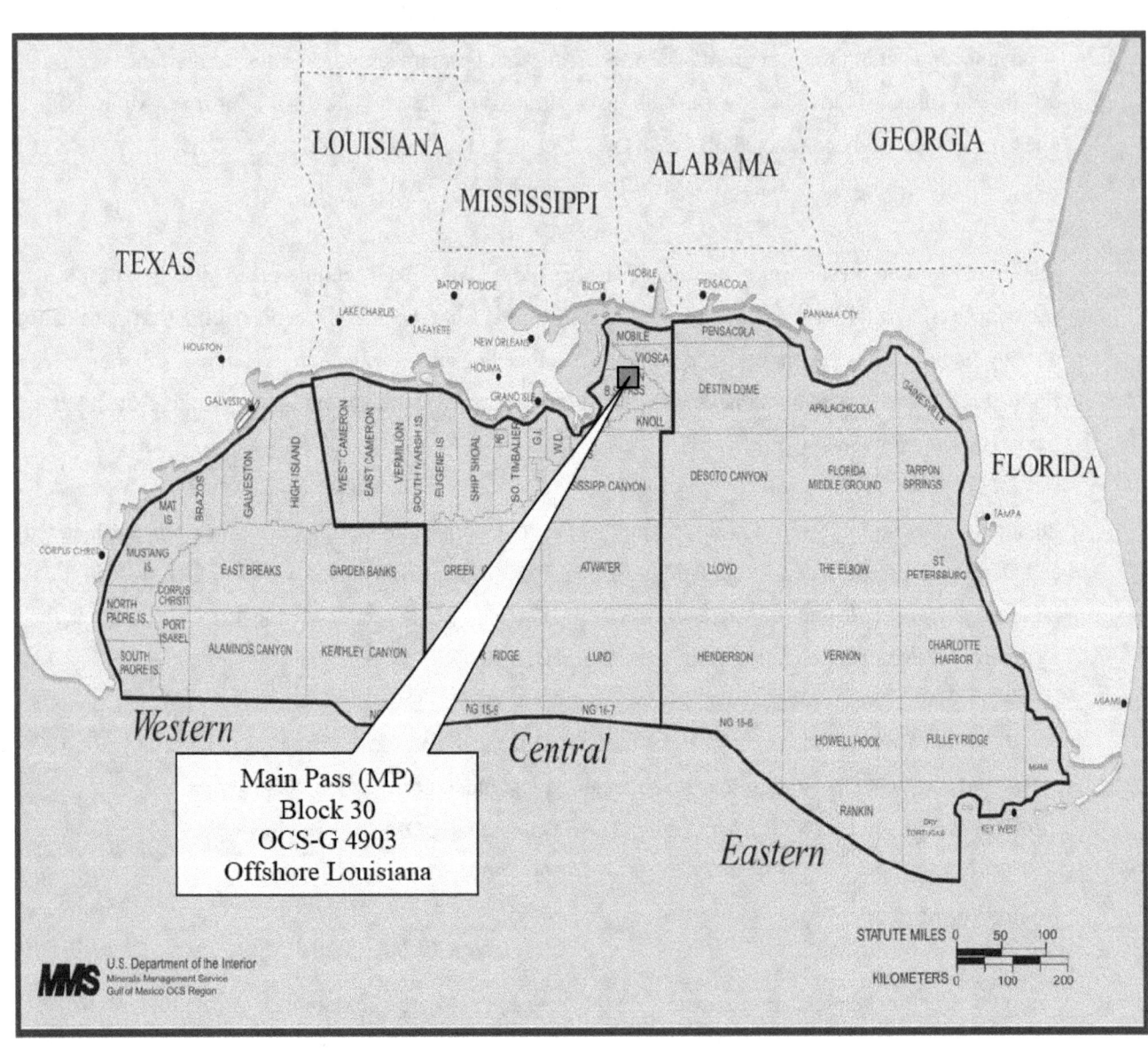

Figure 1: Location of Lease OCS-G 4903, Main Pass Block 30, Offshore Louisiana

Findings

Rig Activities – Timeline through the Accident

The following timeline includes the activities from the rig's move on location to the USCG medi-vac transport of the victim (*see Table 1*).

Date	Activities
TABLE 1	
Rig Activities Timeline from rig on location to USCG medi-vac transport of the victim	
Date	**Activities**
	Rig tow to location and rig-up on MP 30 A platform
March 3-7, 2009	Rig 120 is towed from MP 41 Well #CC-49 to MP 30 A Platform Well #A-14 ST01, the rig floor skidded over the A Platform with stairways, cat walks, V-door installed and rig leveling completed.
March 7, 2009	**Bulk Hose Lifting Operation**
(2100 – 2130 hours)	The VETCO representative conducts an approximately 15-20 minutes formal pre-job written JSA/safety meeting followed by the Driller's verbal lift operation safety meeting. The VETCO representative's JSA Form and safety meeting are limited to specific tasks/hazards associated with only the casing annulus pressure test and not the hose lift operation. The rig crew initiates the air-operated hoist hose lifting operation. The Driller deems the hose lifting connection consisting of a braided sling rigged with a choker to be unsafe and informs the lift crew to replace the sling. The Driller has the crew replace the sling connection to one using a female WECO Figure 1502 hammer union that had been previously modified to include a welded bale. The modified hammer union is then attached to a male double threaded WECO crossover which in turn is made-up to the female WECO union on the 2-inch hose. As the hose is lowered to the well deck from the rig floor it is discovered that the 50 feet of hose assembly failed to reach the well's 13-3/8 inch x 9-7/8 inch casing valve by approximately 10 feet.
(2158 hours)	In the process of replacing the 50 feet of hose with 100 feet of hose, the hose assembly falls from approximately 30 feet from within the derrick to the rig floor

	before continuing its descent into the GOM. FH-1, near the center of the rig floor but not directly under the load, is struck on the hardhat by the hose assembly to sustain life threatening injuries (unresponsive but breathing). FH-2 is knocked down by the hose, arises to be knocked down again by the hoist wire rope that backlashes subsequent to the load being dropped. FH-2 sustains a superficial laceration to his right triceps with minimal right shoulder pain. FH-2 does not require immediate medical attention. FH-2 immediately contacts the Night Tool Pusher (NTP) and Medic from the rig floor Driller's station.
(2200 hours)	The Contract Dispatcher determines from the rig floor monitor and intercom message that FH-1 is lying on the rig floor with serious injuries and immediately contacts Chevron's lead pilot in Venice, LA. While on hold, the Contract Dispatcher is notified by the pilot that the New Orleans USCG has been notified as well as the Plaquemines Parish Sheriff's Office. The New Orleans USCG then notifies the Contract Dispatcher that a USCG medi-vac helicopter has been dispatched from the New Orleans Alvin-Calendar Field. At 2230 hours the Contract Dispatcher continues to address questions from the Plaquemines Parish 911 Dispatcher, Chevron, the USCG and Occupational Safety and Health Administration (OSHA) representatives.
(2201 hours)	The Medic arrives on the rig floor to immobilize the victim's head with c-collar, applies gauze to the head wounds while administering compression and oxygen by bag valve mask and utilizes a modified jaw thrust maneuver to open the airway. FH-1 was then secured to a spine board and carried by crew members to the rig's day room where the Medic continued treatments of intravenous (IV) fluids and oxygen.
(2337 hours)	USCG Helicopter Flight Rescue arrives. FH-1 is carried in the spine board up the rig's port side access stairs into the helicopter.
(2347 hours)	The helicopter departs with the two (2) USCG personnel, FH-1 and the rig Medic to the New Orleans University Hospital. The IV is continued during transport, with Cardio Pulmonary Resuscitation (CPR) required by the Medic approximately seven (7) minutes from the Hospital.
March 8, 2009	FH-1 pronounced deceased by the emergency room trauma team at 0024 hours.

Pre-Job JSA/Safety Meetings

The contract VETCO representative, responsible for overseeing the wellhead's 13-3/8 inch x 9-7/8 inch casing annulus pressure testing operation, conducted a formal pre-job written JSA rig floor safety meeting with all appropriate personnel using a Hercules Offshore JSA Form. The JSA Form and safety meeting reviewed the specific tasks related to only the 13-3/8-inch x 9-7/8-inch casing annulus pressure testing operation. The review included gathering proper tools and the use of Personal Protection Equipment (PPE), removing fittings, opening the casing valve, installing fittings and the use of Stop Work Authority (SWA). The JSA Form was signed by the drilling lift crew, but was not signed by the Night Tool Pusher as he was off-tour at the time of the pre-job JSA safety meeting.

The Driller presented a pre-job rig floor lift safety meeting with all appropriate personnel but a formal JSA was not utilized during the meeting. Subsequent to the accident it was the Driller's opinion that the pre-job safety meeting's verbal discussion should be documented onto the JSA Form. That discussion included making-up a braided rope sling (which was replaced with the modified hammer union connection) on the hose, lifting the hose assembly and lowering same over the hand rail, slacking-off to the platform and tying end of hose to hand rail prior to disconnecting air hoist. The post-accident JSA Form was signed by all appropriate parties including the Hercules Offshore Night Tool Pusher. The Tool Pusher's signature was used to acknowledge reference to the verbal safety meeting discussion that was now being recorded post-accident on the JSA Form. No attempt was made by any individual to hide the fact that the JSA Form was completed and signed by all parties post-accident.

In addition to the specific hose lifting operation the following formal written JSAs were prepared from the rig skid to the hose lifting operation. The JSAs identified the job steps for the operation being analyzed, potential hazards for each job step, hazard reduction measures for each potential hazard and additional Personal Protection Equipment (PPE) as required. Each JSA properly identifies the Supervisor and includes the appropriate team members' signatures.

9

TABLE 2	
JSA's Completed by Activity	
2009 **JSA Date**	**Operation Analyzed**
March 5:	Skidding rig
	Transferring fuel from boat
	Leveling derrick
March 6:	Hanging stairs from rig to platform
	Transferring personnel using crane and personnel basket
	Skidding rig
	Removing shunt line
March 7:	Transferring personnel in man-riding equipment
	Rope attachment to legs
	Skidding rig floor
	Rig jacking
	Transferring personnel using crane and personnel basket
March 8:	Utilization of the air-operated hoist
	Transferring personnel utilizing the crane and personnel basket

Duplicate typed JSAs occur for the skidding rig and transferring personnel utilizing the crane and personnel basket. JSA operations involving rig jacking, hanging stairs from rig to platform, removing shunt line, transferring personnel in man-riding equipment, transferring fuel from boat, rope attachment to legs, preparing and skidding rig floor and leveling derrick occur as individual JSAs. All but three (3) of the total fourteen (14) JSAs are typed with the 3 hand-written JSAs being leveling derrick, hanging stairs from rig to platform and utilization of the air-operated hoist. Members of the drilling hose lift crew were involved in six (6) of the 14 total JSAs. The JSAs are referred to in the daily International Association of Drilling Contractors (IADC) and the morning drilling reports.

Bulk Hose Lifting Operation

The rig's air-operated hoist was being utilized to position 50 feet of 2-inch rubber hose assembly weighing approximately 400 pounds from the rig floor to the well located on the A Platform's wellhead deck. FH-1 was located at approximately the center of the rig floor but not directly under the load. FH-2 was positioned next to the rig floor railing adjacent to the V-door and the Hoist Operator was operating the air-operated hoist at the time of accident (*see Figure 2*). The Driller was assisting with the operation from the rig's pipe deck near the V-door (*see Figures 3 and 4*).

Figure 2: Location of Hercules Rig Floor Hands and Hoist Operator during accident

Figure 3: Location of Driller on rig deck beneath edge of rig floor and above wellhead deck

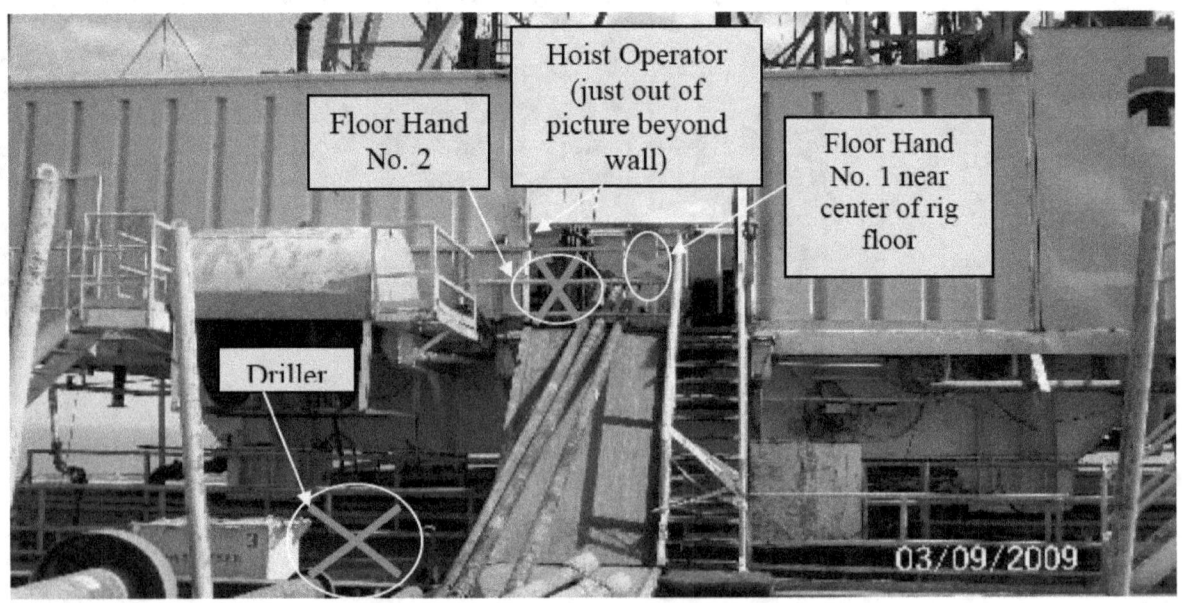

Figure 4: Another view of Driller's location in relation to rig floor

12

The bulk hose assembly was being suspended by the rig floor air-operated hoist in order that the hose's lower end could be connected to the 13-3/8 inch x 9-7/8 inch well's casing annulus valve located on the platform's wellhead deck and the hose's upper end connected to the rig floor manifold. As the lifting operation was initiated, the Driller required the lift crew replace the bridled sling rigged with a choker because he believed this lifting connection arrangement was not safe. The lifting connection then consisted of a WECO Figure 1502 hammer union that had been previously modified by the addition of a welded bale. The WECO Figure 1502 hammer union was then attached to a male double threaded WECO crossover made-up to the female WECO union on the 2-inch hose. The hose assembly's lower end consisted of a female WECO union.

During the latter stage of lowering the hose assembly for connection to the 13-3/8 inch x 9-7/8 inch casing annulus valve, it was determined that the hose failed to reach the casing annulus valve by approximately 10 feet. It was at this time that FH-1 who was at the rig floor hand rail maneuvering the hose swapped-out with FH-2 in order to relieve FH-1 of the hose manipulation duties. The Hoist Operator then began to retrieve the hose assembly back into the derrick above the rig floor where it could be swapped-out with 100 feet of hose section that was located on one wall of the rig floor. When the 50 feet of hose assembly was lifted approximately 30 feet into the derrick above the rig floor, the modified WECO Figure 1502 hammer union's welded bale failed on one end just above the weld (*see Figure 5*) resulting in the hose assembly to fall from the positive safety hook (*see Figure 6*). For comparison purposes a manufactured drill collar lifting sub photo was taken during the accident investigation to outline construction differences in these two different lifting apparatus (*see Figure 7*).

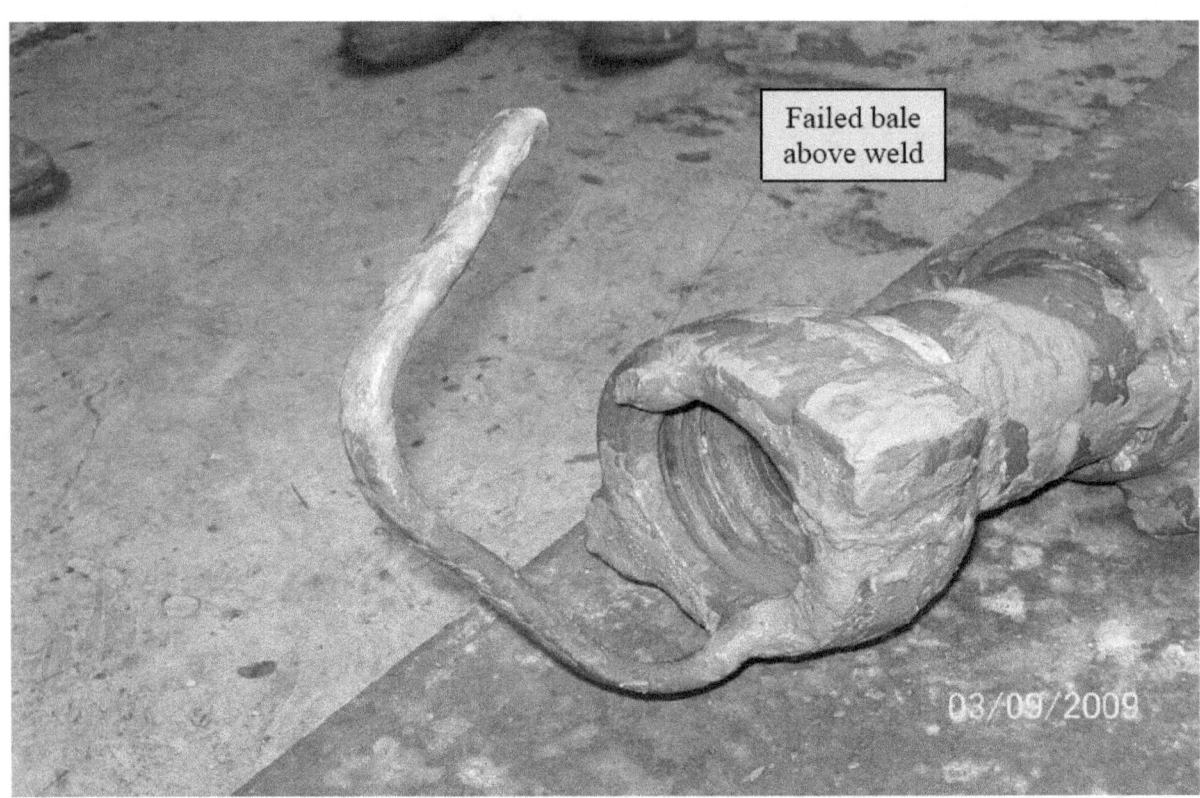

Failed bale
above weld

03/09/2009

Figure 5: Recovered modified WECO Figure 1502 hammer union with failed welded bale

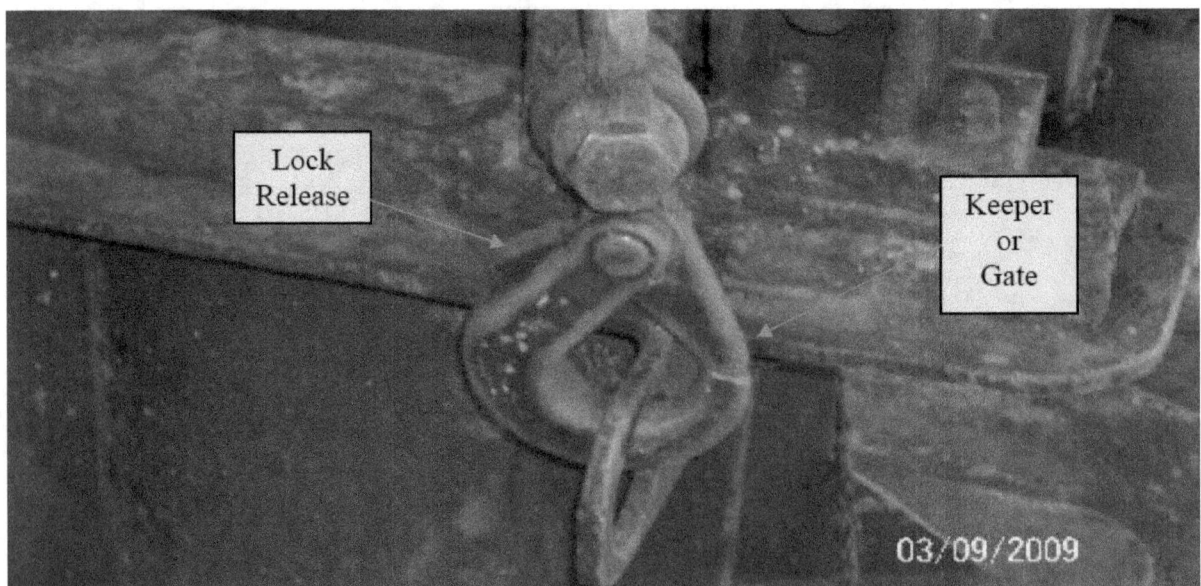

Lock
Release

Keeper
or
Gate

03/09/2009

Figure 6: Safety Hook

14

Figure 7: Manufactured drill collar lift sub taken from the rig floor

Subsequent to bale failure the hose assembly fell to the rig floor resulting in the accident, prior to continuing its descent between the rig floor and wellhead deck into the GOM. Recovered hose assembly photos refer to the photos taken subsequent to the diver recovery operation on 10 March 2009. The recovered hose assembly's female WECO union lower end is shown (*see Figure 8*). Once the lower hose assembly had been properly connected to the well's casing valve, the modified WECO Figure 1502 hammer union would have been replaced with manifold piping (*see Figure 9*) that would be connected from the top of the hose assembly to the rig floor's manifold. The well's 13-3/8-inch x 9-7/8-inch casing annulus would then be pressure tested utilizing the cement pump prior to initiating sidetracking operations.

Subsequent to FH-1 being struck by the modified WECO Figure 1502 hammer connection, FH-2 was knocked down by the hose, arises to be knocked down again by the hoist wire rope that backlashes subsequent to the load being dropped (*see Figure 10*).

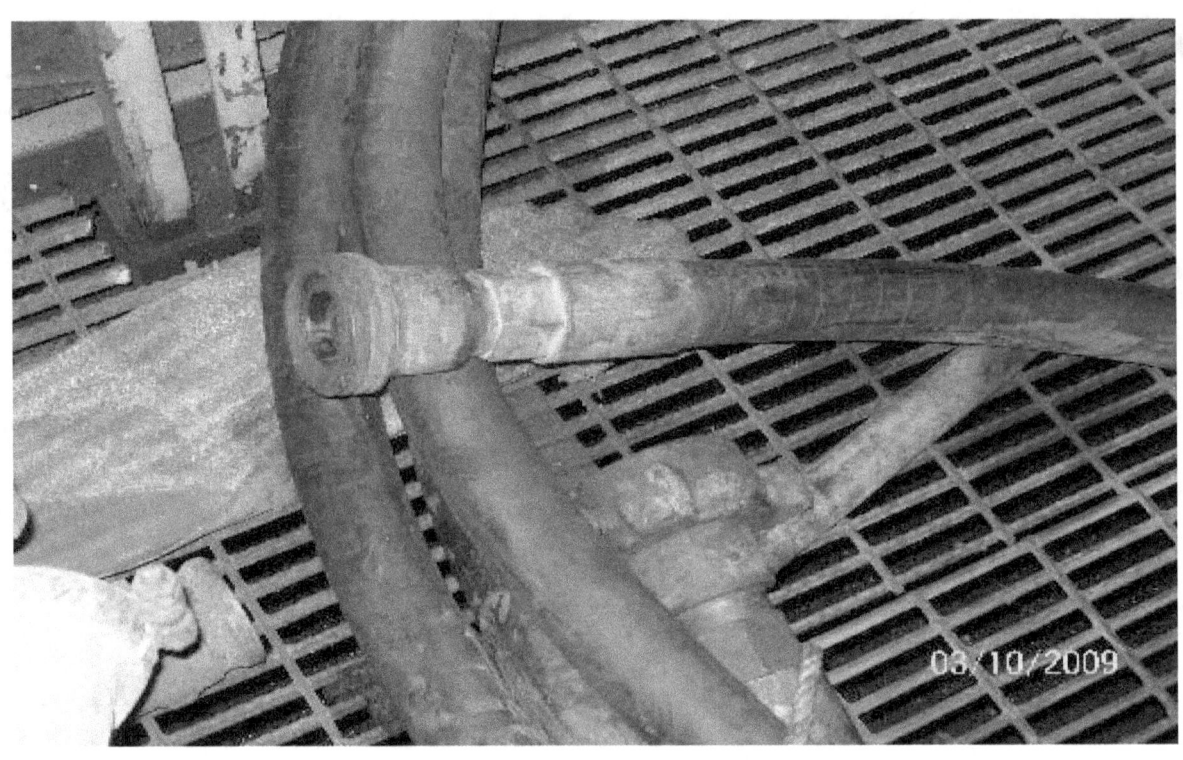

Figure 8: Recovered lower end of hose assembly to be connected to 13-3/8 inch x 9-7/8 inch casing annulus valve

Figure 9: Manifold piping to be connected from the top of hose assembly to the rig floor manifold for pressure testing the 13-3/8 inch x 9-7/8 inch casing annulus

Figure 10: Air-operated hoist back-lashed wire rope
(Subsequent to the dropped hose assembly)

Post Accident Events

Subsequent to the accident, FH-1 was immediately treated on the rig floor by the rig Medic. FH-1 was then secured to and carried in a spine board by crew members to the rig's day room where the Medic continued oxygen treatments while initiating Intravenous (IV) fluids. All proper notifications were made by the rig's Contract Dispatcher, and in approximately 2 hours the victim was being transported by a USCG Helicopter Flight Rescue to the New Orleans University Hospital. FH-1 was pronounced deceased by the emergency trauma team at 0024 hours on 8 March 2009.

Hercules Post-Accident Offshore HSE Bulletin

On 11 March 2009 the Hercules Offshore Vice President of Operations Worldwide posted a Safety Notice to all Hercules Offshore Installation Managers (OIMs) and Operations Management. Listed below is a synopsis of the immediate action items to be implemented:

- Rig crews including supervisors will conduct a detailed inspection "Hazard Hunt" of all rig areas/spaces, including tool storage areas and storage lockers to look for and collect non-approved/non-certified lifting gear that may be onboard.
- Emphasis will be placed on loose lifting gear "hardware" that is homemade/rig fabricated.
- If non-certified lifting gear/hardware is found during the Hazard Hunt, it will be immediately removed from service and destroyed to ensure it is never used for lifting or any other purpose.
- Crews will be instructed on the importance of risk assessing and visually inspecting each rigging/load lifting arrangement for safety. Rig Management will ensure that all crewmembers know that homemade/rig fabricated lifting hardware/equipment is prohibited with no exceptions.
- This Policy will be implemented upon receipt of this bulletin or As Soon As Possible (ASAP).
- OIMs will report completion of this requirement to Rig Management and document compliance of the loose lifting gear Hazard Hunt by comments on the Morning Drilling Report.

Hercules Offshore Lifting Personnel Testimony

The day following the accident thirty-eight (38) onsite written statements were recorded by representatives of the New Orleans law firm LeBlanc Bland P.L.L.C., a third party firm requested by Hercules Offshore to perform the preliminary investigation. These statements were used by the Panel members to select personal interviews with three (3) drilling lift crew members: the Driller, Hoist Operator and FH-2. These interviews were conducted by the Panel at the New Orleans MMS OCS GOM Regional office on 14 April 2009 and attended by the USCG and a representative from LeBlanc Bland P.L.L.C. There was a consistent theme throughout the interview process with key components of that interview session outlined below:

- All interviews were consistent with the written statements.

- The VETCO representative's pre-job written JSA/safety meeting was performed, with discussion as outlined in the Pre-Job JSA/Safety Meetings section of the Panel report, just prior to the Driller's pre-job verbal safety meeting and attended by all appropriate members that signed the Hercules Offshore JSA Form.

- The Driller's pre-job verbal safety meeting, with discussion as outlined in the Pre-Job JSA/Safety Meetings section of the Panel report, was performed immediately following the VETCO JSA/safety meeting, immediately prior to initiating the lift operation and attended by all appropriate personnel that signed the post-accident Hercules Offshore JSA Form.

- Two of the three members believed that the Chevron Company Man was in attendance for the VETCO pre-job/JSA safety meeting, with none confirming attendance by the Company Man during the Driller's verbal pre-job safety meeting.

- The modified hammer union connection was identified by all as being on the rig as long as each of the members were assigned to the rig, with five (5) years as being the greatest length of rig service time. None of the members knew where or by whom the hammer union modification was made nor if any load capacity testing or other certification was performed.

- The modified hammer union connection had been previously used for similar hose assembly lifts with the hose lifts being the heaviest lifts. Other lifts utilizing the modified hammer union included smaller components; e.g., chicksen joints, smaller low-torque valves, etc.

- This type of bulk hose lifting operation was construed as being a standard or normal lift that would not require a written JSA under the Hercules Offshore HSE JSA policy.

- The modified hammer union connection would normally be hand threaded during initial make-up, but then a hammer used to tighten the connection prior to initiating the lifts.

- None of the members could identify the Hercules Offshore individual(s) responsible for inspecting the lift equipment, although all were aware of a formal inspection program.

- When asked what lifting procedures could be done differently for future lifts, all members were in agreement that the modified hammer union or a similar modified lift component should not be used during future lifting operations.

- FH-1 was initially involved in manipulating the hose from the rig floor hand rail during the lowering phase of the hose operation, but FH-2 swapped-out with FH-1 during the hose assembly's lifting phase prior to the accident. FH-1 and FH-2 each participated as Signalers during the time they were standing at the rig floor hand rail in communication with the Driller who also served as a Signaler during the blind bulk hose lift operation.

- The Hoist Operator and FH-2 did not believe FH-1 was performing an essential job function at the time of the accident, but knew that FH-1 was standing by to assist with replacing the 50 feet of hose assembly with the 100 feet of hose section. The Driller could not be sure of FH-1's job function at the time of the accident because the Driller was located on the rig's pipe deck out of sight from FH-1.

Review of Rigger Training Certificates and Crew Logistics

The Panel reviewed the lift crew's Hercules Offshore Rigger Training records to determine:

Employee	Certificate Rigger Training Certification Date	Certificate Rigger Training Expiration Date
Driller	12/12/2003	None Provided
Hoist Operator	11/07/2006	11/07/2010
FH-1	06/18/2005	06/18/2007
FH-2	12/19/2006	12/19/2010

The Hoist Operator and FH-2 Rigger Training certificates indicate that both individuals are certified until 2010. The FH-1 certificate's expiration date was 18 June 2007, with no certificate expiration date indicated for the Driller. Several lift assist devices (e.g., stiff legs, hydraulic masts, air-operated hoists) currently fall outside the rigger refresher training requirement of at least every four (4) years under the scope of American Petroleum Institute (API) Recommend Practice (RP) 2D, Fifth Edition, June 2003 titled "*Operation and Maintenance of Offshore Cranes*".

According to Hercules Offshore Lifting Gear Policy, employees that are required to sling and move loads with material handling equipment must receive specified training from line supervisors on the job or from a third-party instructor hired to provide Rigger Training. As per the Hercules Offshore Mechanical/Hoisting Operation Policy, Rigger Training certificates are required onsite and current.

Chevron's GOM Business Units Shelf and Deepwater Contractor's Handbook (Chevron's Handbook) - Revised January 2008

Chevron's Handbook provides guidance and a minimum set of expectations for Chevron and Contractor employees regarding contractor work performed under Chevron's operational control. Contractors are required to follow the policies and procedures established by the Contractor's company in addition to any Chevron site-specific policies. The Contractor is obligated to become familiar with and follow the contents of Chevron's Handbook, and if Chevron's Handbook procedures and the Contractor's procedures conflict, the more stringent rule should be followed.

Pertinent Chevron Handbook Lift Policy/Sections

Section 2.2 (Contractor Responsibilities): "...*read, become familiar with, and follow the contents of the Handbook... These guidelines are intended to supplement, not replace, the contractor's own safety program. If Chevron's procedures and the contractor's procedures conflict, the more stringent rule should be followed*".

Section 5.2 (Pre-Job HSE Meetings): "*Before a new job, at the beginning of each workday, or in the event of a significant operational change, the PIC must hold a pre-job meeting to discuss job planning, job assignments, the completion of a written JSA, and any unique or unusual project hazards...*"

Section 17.1.1 (Job Safety Analysis): "*The contractor is required to perform JSAs before each job, including all crane lifts. JSAs must assess each aspect of the task and identify items that could pose a threat to the environment or result in injury to personnel or damage to equipment. All JSA documents should include at least the following:*
- *List of job tasks, which must be written out, not-pre-filled out on the form. Certain non-complex jobs may not require a written JSA, but if uncertain, the Contractor should check with the Chevron PIC.*
- *List of related safety, health, and environmental hazards associated with each task.*
- *Mitigation strategies for each hazard identified, including a check of any PPE to be used.*
- *Assignment of accountability for mitigation.*

- *Signature of supervisor and all participants.*

Other requirements for conducting a JSA include:
- *Involvement of any other Chevron employees or Contractors who may be affected by the Contractor's work when preparing the Contractor's JSA.*
- *Single-person crews performing a task where the task does not affect others must review the JSA with the Chevron representative, or their supervisor, before starting work.*
- *Stopping work when events or conditions change from the original plan and reviewing/revising the plan with all parties involved. Additionally, if new personnel arrive at the site after the job or activities have begun; those personnel will review the JSA before beginning work. If a Contractor request that the JSA be signed off by the Chevron PIC, that person will sign his/her name to the top of the document with JSA performed."*

Hercules Offshore HSE Manual – August 2007

The Hercules Offshore HSE Manual identifies policies to clearly identify and establish minimum health, safety, and environmental standards when conducting work operations aboard Hercules Offshore installations, vessels and facilities. Pertinent lift related sections of the HSE Manual are addressed below in order to assist the Panel in addressing safety related issues associated with the accident's lifting operation.

Pertinent Hercules Offshore HSE Manual Lift Policy/Sections

Pertinent Sections have been identified by Policy Number as follows:
- Policy No. HSE 100.11 (Job Safety Analysis):
  Section 3.1: *"It is the responsibility of the OIM/PIC/Facility manager to ensure that personnel perform a task-specific Job Safety Analysis (JSA) prior to starting jobs that have multiple or complex steps, known hazards with a "possible or probable" likelihood of causing an incident, or have the potential to cause incidents of high severity".*

Section 3.2: "*Jobs that have a low or "remote" likelihood of experiencing an incident and would involve a low potential severity if an incident occurred may not require completion of a formal JSA*".

Section 4.2: "*The benefit of the JSA process resides in the work group discussion of job planning, hazard identification, risk reduction, learning, and understanding. The JSA Form #SAF-05 captures the learning of the risk assessment discussion for reference at the job site and for reference when planning the next job... Note: Simply printing a copy of an existing JSA and reading it aloud is not acceptable risk assessment. Job hazards must be discussed with focus on improving and updating the content of the JSA. Each time a job is performed something will be different. Equipment used, weather conditions, time of day, or experience of crewmembers will never be identical and such differences must be captured*".

➢ Policy No. HSE 100.20 (Lifting Gear):

Section 4.0: "*Homemade or modified lifting equipment shall never be used*".

Section 4.4: "*Slings and lifting gear are safety critical. Failure of this equipment exposes us to high severity personal harm and property damage incidents. If something looks wrong during inspection of lifting gear and rigging of loads, always err on the side of safety and ask a supervisor. If still in doubt, always err on the side of safety by destroying damaged rigging equipment and obtaining the correct gear to safely rig the load.*"

Section 4.7: "*Loose lifting gear consists of hooks, shackles, lifting eyes, pad eyes, or other hardware necessary to connect and sling loads being lifted. Loose gear must be inspected for cracks, stretching, and bending of steel. Checking for excessive wear, rust, or other forms of damage must also be considered during inspection. Hardware involved with a lift must be checked to ensure it has a proper Maximum Safe Working Load (SWL) rating. Proof load certificates must also be maintained for loose lifting gear in use and details included in the Lifting Gear Register.*"

Section 4.7.4: "*Slings with sliding choker hooks shall not be used because of the open sliding hooking possibly losing hold if tension is released. Using a double wrap choker hitch will reduce the hazard. If moving bundles of pipe, the double wrap choker hitch can be bull dogged with a wire rope clip to maintain tension on the bundle when it is landed."*

Section 4.9: *"Employees that are required to sling and move loads with material handling equipment must receive training from line supervisors on the job or from a third-party instructor hired to provide rigger training."*

➤ Policy No. HSE 100.21 (Mechanical/Hoisting Operations):
Section 4.2.5: *"Lifts that involve blind spots require that a stand-alone Signalman/Banksman is assigned to oversee the safety on the lift and give hand signals. This person shall not be involved with the rigging/handling of the load being moved."*

Section 4.2.6: *"Tag lines, free of knots and of proper lengths, shall be attached to all lifts. When two tag lines are required, they shall be controlled from the same side of the load."*

Section 4.2.8: *"Persons rigging/slinging loads shall remain in a position of safety and have an escape route."*

Section 4.2.9: *"Personnel not involved in the lifting operation or the JSA shall stay clear of the lift area in a position of safety."*

Section 4.2.10: *"Personnel shall never stand or walk under suspended loads or allow a load to be swung over their head"*.

Section 4.2.11: *"Riggers attempting to spot loads shall avoid placing hands on the load and stand clear until tag lines are accessible (load approximately waist high)."*

Section 4.2.14: *"All lifting equipment and hardware must be certified of adequate SWL and visually inspected for condition prior to being used for overhead lifting."*

<u>Section 4.3.3</u>: "*Personnel working in the movement area of an air hoist/tugger must be aware of the intended path of the load being moved and remain in a position of safety in case of dropped objects or wire failure*".

<u>Section 4.5</u>: "*Miscellaneous lifting appliances include chain falls, come-a-long, air spider baskets, portable jacks, or other devices capable of lifting, holding tension, or suspending loads. This equipment shall be maintained and inspected as per manufacturer's recommendations and will be included in the Preventive Maintenance System....*"

Conclusions

The Accident

It is the conclusion of the Panel that during the night of 7 March 2009 as 50 feet of bulk hose assembly was lifted approximately 30 feet into the derrick above the rig floor, the modified WECO Figure 1502 hammer union, being utilized as the lift connection, failed just above the weld on one end of the bale to result in the hose assembly falling and fatally striking one Floorhand while injuring another Floorhand. FH-1 standing near the center of the rig floor but not directly under the assembly, received life threatening injuries (unresponsive but breathing) and was pronounced deceased approximately two hours later subsequent to being struck on the top of his hardhat by the hose assembly. FH-2, standing next to the rig floor hand railing and manipulating the load from snagging on any protrusions, was initially knocked down by the hose, then later by the air-operated hoist wire rope, to sustain a superficial laceration to his right triceps with right shoulder pain.

Cause

Modified Lift Connection:

1. It is the conclusion of the Panel that, as the hose assembly was being lifted, the use of a modified WECO Figure 1502 hammer union resulted in failure just above the weld on one end of the welded bale.

The Panel was unable to ascertain when or by whom the hammer union had been modified, but from interview testimony learned that the modified union was located on the rig at least five (5) years. Hercules Offshore Policy Number HSE 100.20 Section 4.1 states that homemade or modified lifting equipment shall never be used. **Therefore, utilization of the modified WECO Figure 1502 hammer union as a lift connection is concluded to be the cause of the accident.**

Possible Contributing Causes

Hercules Offshore Equipment Inspection Program:

1. It is the conclusion of the Panel that the Hercules Offshore equipment inspection program was not properly implemented and monitored to prevent equipment modification and the use of modified equipment for lifting. Although witness testimony indicated employee awareness of an inspection program, testimony was unable to ascertain by whom or how frequently the equipment inspection was performed.

Hercules Offshore Policy Number HSE 100.20 Section 4.7 states that hardware involved with a lift must be checked to ensure it has a proper maximum safe working load rating. Hercules Offshore Policy Number HSE 100.21 Section 4.2.14 also states that all lifting equipment and hardware must be certified of adequate maximum safe working load rating and its condition visually inspected prior to being used for overhead lifting. Hercules Offshore requires that proof load certificates be maintained for loose lifting gear in use and details included in the Hercules Offshore Lifting Gear Register.

Prior to utilization of the modified hammer union as a lift connection, no load capacity testing or other certification could be confirmed. In addition, there was no way to determine how many times the hammer union bale may have been fatigued by poor handling practices; e.g., striking the bale with a hammer during make-up, dropping/bending the bale during previous lifts, etc. **Therefore, the improper implementation and monitoring of the Hercules Offshore equipment inspection program is concluded to be a contributing cause of the incident**.

Lift Crew Location during the Bulk Hose Lifting Operation:

1. It is the conclusion of the Panel that, as a result of location of rig floor space limiting the use of rig floor barriers, the length and angle of the hoisted hose assembly in conjunction with the speed of the falling load, the location of the lift crew played a crucial role.

Testimony indicates that FH-1 at the time of the accident was most likely not performing an essential job function from his position on the rig floor. Hercules Offshore Policy Number HSE 100.21 Section 4.2.9

states that personnel not involved in the lifting operation shall stay clear of the lift area in a position of safety. Although FH-1 was near the center of the rig floor but not directly under the load, he remained within the load's potential fall path as a result of the angle of the hose fall. FH-2 was also within the load's potential fall path as a result of having to physically manipulate the hose by hand. Hercules Offshore Policy Number HSE 100.21 Section 4.2.8 states that persons rigging/slinging loads shall remain in a position of safety and have an escape route. It so happened that the Hoist Operator, although within the load's potential fall path and possible whipping action of the hose, was not injured by the hose assembly or the air-operated hoist's back-lashed wire rope. The bulk hose lifting operation did have the potential for additional injuries as a result of personnel location. **Therefore, the lift crew's location on the rig floor is concluded to be a possible cause of the incident.**

JSA Form:

1. It is the conclusion of the Panel that, although a pre-job rig floor lift safety meeting was conducted, the lack of a formal JSA lift document implies the possibility of lost opportunities for the exchange of vital information. The use of a written JSA protocol is usually more specific than a safety meeting alone in addressing each sequence of the basic job steps and the potential hazards and recommended action or controls necessary for controlling the hazard.

Hercules Offshore Policy Number HSE 100.11 Section 4.2 states that the benefits of the JSA process resides in the work group's discussion of job planning, hazard identification, risk reduction, learning and understanding. It also outlines that the JSA Form captures the learning of the risk assessment discussion for reference at the job site and when planning the job. Section 4.2 further states that a JSA shall be developed from scratch for any particular job that has never had a written JSA performed, because simply printing a copy of an existing JSA and reading it is not acceptable risk assessment. The Section continues to state that each time a job is performed, something will be different; e.g., equipment used, weather conditions, time of day, or experience of crewmembers never being identical and such differences must be captured. Although a formal JSA Form was completed by the Driller post-accident, the Panel concludes that, although done without any intentional cover-up, this was the incorrect time to document what should have been documented and utilized prior to initiating the lifting operation. The Panel concludes that many workers do not understand that it is not the JSA Form alone that will keep them safe on the job but rather the process the JSA represents. **Therefore, the lack of a formal JSA during the**

pre-job rig floor lift verbal discussion is concluded to be a possible cause of the incident by not having allowed for possible opportunities of higher levels of risk assessment associated with the air-operated lift tasks rather than the task risks being reduced to As Low as Reasonably Practicable (ALARP).

JSA Policy Oversight by Rig Management:

1. It is the conclusion of the Panel that, lack of a formal JSA document during the pre-job rig floor safety meeting implies: (a) an absence of the Contractor's commitment to Chevron's Contractor Handbook JSA policy and (b) the apparent failure on the part of Chevron to provide the necessary oversight to ensure that formal JSA protocol be followed prior to the bulk hose lifting operation.

Chevron's Handbook Sections 5.2 and 17.1.1 specifically addresses the need for a written JSA and pre-job safety meeting before a new job, at the beginning of each workday and in the event of a significant operational change, in addition to the minimal JSA documentation requirements including a pre-job safety meeting. Hercules Offshore Policy Number HSE 100.11 Section 3.2 identifies that jobs having a low or remote likelihood of experiencing an incident and would involve a low potential severity if an incident occurred may not require completion of a formal JSA. The Panel concluded that a formal written JSA pre-job safety meeting, therefore, was not conducted by the lift crew as a result of the Driller's decision that the "standard" or "routine" nature of the lift operation complied with the Policy. Hercules Offshore Policy Number HSE 100.11 Section 3.1 states it is the responsibility of the OIM/PIC/Facility Manager to ensure that personnel perform a task-specific JSA prior to starting jobs that have multiple or complex steps, know hazards with a "possible or probable" likelihood of causing an incident, or have the potential to cause incidents of high severity. The Hercules Offshore Night tool Pusher did sign the JSA Form, but only after the Form was completed post-accident to indicate his concurrence with documenting the verbal pre-job lift safety meeting. Neither the Night Tool Pusher nor the Company Man was present at the time of the Driller's verbal pre-job safety meeting.

Chevron's Handbook Section 2.2 identifies that contractors become familiar with and follow the contents of the Handbook while also stating that if Chevron's procedures and the contractor's procedures conflict, the more stringent rule should be followed. It is the conclusion of the Panel that Chevron's Handbook JSA policies supersede the Hercules Offshore JSA policy and a formal JSA should have been utilized during the pre-job rig floor safety meeting. **Therefore, the lack of JSA oversight by rig management is concluded to be a possible cause of the incident.**

Recommendations

The investigative Panel recommends that the MMS should issue two Safety Alerts to industry regarding this accident. One Safety Alert should briefly describe the accident and identify all the causes with the following recommendations made:

- *Non-approved/non-certified (homemade/field manufactured) lifting equipment should be immediately removed from service (discarded) and immediately brought to management's attention.*

- *In order for lift equipment inspection/maintenance programs to be effective, Operators and their Contractors should:*
  - *Include visual inspections prior to use.*
  - *Properly clean, grease and/or oil equipment after each use.*
  - *Ensure that the lifting component is used only in accordance with the manufacturer's specifications and instructions for use.*
  - *Replace the equipment when it exceeds the manufacturer's recommended use.*

MMS has previously issued Safety Alert Number 276 titled Job Safety Analysis (JSA), which recommends to Operators when and how they should conduct a JSA. This Safety Alert does not specifically state that Operators and their Contractors should review each others HSE JSA Policies to determine if JSA's are required for all types of lifting operations and not just those operations deemed "critical" or "unusual". Therefore, this investigative Panel recommends that MMS review and re-issue Safety Alert Number 276 to recommend:

  - *Operator's and their Contractors review and communicate their respective HSE JSA policies to determine if a formal written JSA and safety meeting are required for lifting or other operations.*
  - *Workers understand that not performing formal written JSA safety meetings provide another opportunity of higher levels of risk associated with operational tasks rather than the tasks being reduced to As Low as Reasonably Practicable (ALARP).*
  - *Workers understand that it is not the JSA Form alone that will keep them safe on the job but rather the process the JSA represents. It is of little value to identify hazards and devise proper controls if the controls are not put in place.*

MMS should consider working with API to develop best practices for the use of, operation, inspection and maintenance of lifting devices.

www.ingramcontent.com/pod-product-compliance
Lightning Source LLC
Chambersburg PA
CBHW052023280526
45793CB00005B/1101